ISBN - 978-0-9917887-4-3

This book was inspired by my beloved mother Elizabeth, and cherished daughter Victoria xo..

Special thanks to Angel Brkic whose artistic talents brought these words to life.

I am so grateful for the love and support of my dear husband Barry, and all my family and friends that encouraged me along the way.

Matlox Publishing

Every morning when Lizzy woke up, she would start her day by saying things like "I don't like the way my hair looks, and my nose is too big, and my cheeks are too fat." Lizzy would look in the mirror and keep saying these things over and over.

When Lizzy would go to school she would say to herself, "I don't get this work, It's too hard, and I am too stupid."

Lizzy would come home, and she would feel tired and sad.

Lizzy's mother would ask her, "Did you have fun at school today?" and Lizzy would say "No!" as loud as she could.

One day Lizzy's mother said, "Come here, I want you to meet our new neighbors. They have a girl about your age." Lizzy came out to the kitchen and there stood a girl with the biggest smile on her face.

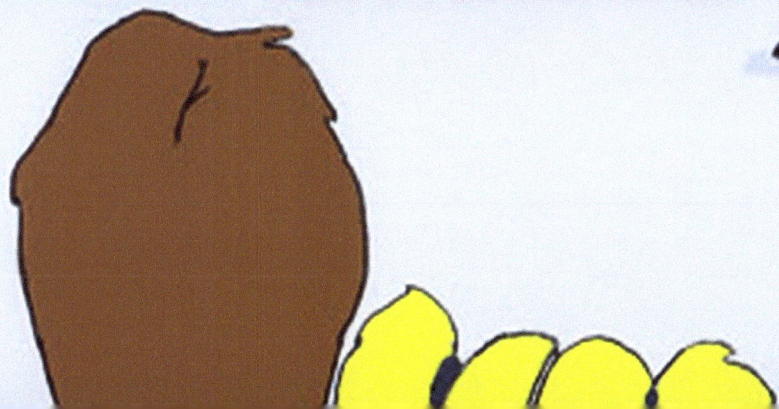

Lizzy said, "Hi" and looked at the floor. The girl said, "Hi Lizzy, I am Victoria and I am so happy that we can be friends." The two girls went to Lizzy's room to play.

Victoria would say, "I am so thankful I met you Lizzy, and that we live so close to each other."Lizzy smiled, she felt the same way too.

It seemed like Victoria was thankful for a lot of things. When they ate dinner Victoria would say she was thankful for the good food she was eating. Lizzy thought about how happy Victoria always seemed to be, and Lizzy wanted to know how she could be that happy too.

Lizzy woke up the next morning and went through all the things she didn't like about herself. She felt sad again, and thought, I am going to find out why Victoria is so happy all the time.

Lizzy went next door, and knocked on the door. Victoria's mother answered and told Lizzy to go upstairs, that Victoria was in her room. As Lizzy walked up the stairs, she heard some music coming from the room.

She stood at the door, and she could hear Victoria shouting over the music. "I Love my hair, I Love my face, I love my house, and I Love my friends." Lizzy opened the door, and stepped inside the room. There was Victoria, jumping on the bed, and shouting about loving everything.

Victoria motioned to Lizzy to join her on the bed, and the two girls jumped and shouted about everything they could possibly think of that they loved.

After doing this for a while, both girls fell on the bed and laughed until they had tears in their eyes.

That night when Lizzy's Mom was tucking her into bed, she asked, "Did you have fun today?" Lizzy had the biggest smile ever as she said "Yes Momma, I had the best time and I now know how to be happy."

Lizzy's Mother listened while Lizzy told her how important it is to be thankful for everything and love everything about yourself. It makes you feel light and happy when you do.

Lizzy's Mom turned out the light, and said "I Love you Lizzy." Lizzy said, I Love you too Momma," and then she whispered to herself, "I Love you Lizzy."

www.ingramcontent.com/pod-product-compliance
Lightning Source LLC
Chambersburg PA
CBHW040231070426
42447CB00030B/152